Victoria

CW00496220

REVISE EDEXCEL
FUNCTIONAL SKILLS ENTRY L
English

REVISION
GUIDE

Series Consultant: Harry Smith
Author: David Grant

A note from the publisher

In order to ensure that this resource offers high-quality support for the associated Pearson qualification, it has been through a review process by the awarding body. This process confirms that this resource fully covers the teaching and learning content of the specification or part of a specification at which it is aimed. It also confirms that it demonstrates an appropriate balance between the development of subject skills, knowledge and understanding, in addition to preparation for assessment.

Endorsement does not cover any guidance on assessment activities or processes (e.g. practice questions or advice on how to answer assessment questions), included in the resource nor does it prescribe any particular approach to the teaching or delivery of a related course.

While the publishers have made every attempt to ensure that advice on the qualification and its assessment is accurate, the official specification and associated assessment guidance materials are the only authoritative source of information and should always be referred to for definitive guidance.

Pearson examiners have not contributed to any sections in this resource relevant to examination papers for which they have responsibility.

Examiners will not use endorsed resources as a source of material for any assessment set by Pearson.

Endorsement of a resource does not mean that the resource is required to achieve this Pearson qualification, nor does it mean that it is the only suitable material available to support the qualification, and any resource lists produced by the awarding body shall include this and other appropriate resources.

Contents

A small bit of small print

Edexcel publishes Sample Assessment Material and the Specification on its website. This is the official content and this book should be used in conjunction with it. The questions in Now try this have been written to help you practise every topic in the book. Remember: the real exam questions may not look like this.

1-to-1
page match with the
Entry Level 3 Revision
Workbook
ISBN 978 129214 573 0

Your reading test

To do well in your Entry Level 3 Functional Skills English qualification, you will need to prepare for your reading test.

Your reading test

You will need to complete **two** tasks worth a total of **20 marks**. Each task contains **two texts** about the same theme or topic. You should answer all the questions for each task.

Planning your time

You will have **45 minutes** to complete your reading test. You are allowed to split this time over more than one session.

Planning your time during the test is very important. Split your time between the two tasks evenly and make sure you have time to check your answers.

Types of question

1   Some of the questions will be **multiple choice**. You will need to put a tick in the box next to the correct answer.

2   Some of the questions will be **short response questions**. You will need to write your own answer.

If you change your mind about an answer, put a line through it and mark or write your new answer.

1 According to Text A1, where should you go to check your car tyre pressure?

   A the petrol station ☐

   B the supermarket ☐

   C a car hire firm ☐

   D the car park ☐

2 Write your answer on the line below.
Look up the word '**guideline**' in your dictionary and write down what it means.

....

Using a dictionary

You could be asked to use a dictionary in the test to find the meaning of a word. You can also use a dictionary to look up the **definition** of any word you do not understand.

Definition *noun*
The exact meaning of a word, found in a dictionary

Go to page 6 for more on using a dictionary.

Now try this

1 How many texts in total will you have to read in the reading test?
2 How many marks is the reading test worth?

Reading the question

Before you answer a question, make sure you know exactly what it is asking.

Following instructions

Below are some of the types of instruction you will find in your reading test.

This means that you must answer questions 1 to 5 with information you find in Text B1.

> **Read Text B1 and answer questions 1 to 5.**

This means you will find the answer to this question in Text B1. It is not asking you what skills **you** think a receptionist should have – it is asking what the **text** says about the skills a receptionist needs.

> **1** According to Text B1, which of these skills should a receptionist have?

You will have a dictionary in the reading test. This question is asking you to use the dictionary to find out what the word means and to write down its meaning.

> **2** Look up the word '**extend**' in your dictionary and write down what it means.

Understanding the question

Read the question two or three times to make sure you understand what you are being asked.

You may find it helpful to try putting the question into your own words.

> According to Text B1, which of these skills should a receptionist have?

> Which of these skills does the text say you will need if you want to get the job as a receptionist?

Now try this

Use the skills you have practised on this page to complete the task below.

Read Text B1 on page 52 and answer questions 1 and 2.

1 Put a tick ☑ in the correct box.

According to Text B1, how can you find out more about the job on offer?

  A   Phone the leisure centre's manager   ☐

  B   Visit the leisure centre's website   ☐

  C   Visit the leisure centre   ☐

  D   Ask a member of staff at the leisure centre   ☐

2 Look up the word '**extend**' in your dictionary and write down what it means.

Finding the main idea

The first thing to do when you are reading a new text is to work out the main idea: what the text is about.

Skim reading

Skim reading the texts in the test will help you to find the key information and identify the main ideas quickly. When you are skim reading, you should focus on key parts of the text, such as:

- titles or headings
- the first sentence of each paragraph
- bold, underlined or highlighted text
- images
- numbers and bullet points.

The introduction

Each of the texts in the test will have a brief introduction, which will tell you what **type of text** you are being asked to read. This might be:

- an email
- a website
- a newsletter
- a poster
- an advert
- a leaflet.

The introduction will also tell you the **purpose** of the text: the reason the writer wrote it.

Finding the main idea of Text A2

Look at the introduction, the title and the opening sentence of Text A2 below (full text on page 51). You can guess from these features that the text is going to be about driving.

Stacey reads the following information on a website about how to drive safely.

This **introduction** tells you that this text is from a **website** and that it will give you **information**.

This **title** tells you that the text is about speed limits.

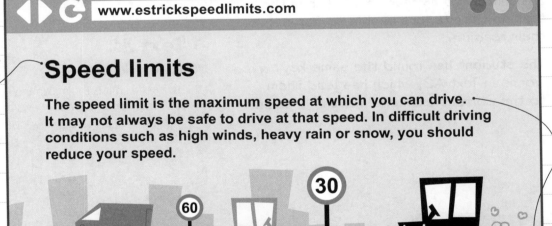

www.estrickspeedlimits.com

Speed limits

The speed limit is the maximum speed at which you can drive. It may not always be safe to drive at that speed. In difficult driving conditions such as high winds, heavy rain or snow, you should reduce your speed.

The **opening sentence** tells you that the text is specifically about speed limits when driving.

Now try this

Look carefully at the introduction, title and opening sentences of Text B1 on page 52.

What clues do they give you about the main idea of Text B1?

Underlining key words

Underlining key words or phrases in the question will help you to find the answer quickly.

What should you underline?

You should only underline key words or phrases that will help you to answer the question.

 Key words in the question

Each question in your test will contain one or more key words or phrases. The key words or phrases in the question are:

- the most important words or phrases
- unlikely to appear very often in the text.

 Key words in the text

When you have found the key word or phrase in the question, you should skim read the text looking for the same or similar key words or phrases.

> Go to page 3 to revise skim reading.

Reading around the key words

When you have found the key word in the text, read around it to find the answer.

Look at a student's underlining on the right.

✓ The student has underlined two important phrases in the question. Words such as 'conditions' and 'reduce' are unlikely to appear very often in the text so the student is able to focus their reading.

✓ The student has found the same key words in Text A2, which has lead them to the correct examples for the answer.

Worked example

According to Text A2, give **two** examples of <u>difficult driving conditions</u> in which drivers should <u>reduce their speed</u>.

high winds and snow

Text A2

Speed limits

The speed limit is the maximum speed at which you can drive. It may not always be safe to drive at that speed. In <u>difficult driving conditions</u> such as high winds, heavy rain or snow, you should <u>reduce your speed</u>.

Now try this

Read the question on the right and Text A1 on page 50.

1 Identify the matching key word(s) or phrase(s) in the text and the question.
2 Answer the question.

> According to Text A1, state **one** thing Stacey should check on her car every month.

Finding details

You will need to find specific information and details in the text to answer the test questions.

Looking for relevant information

Think carefully about what information you are being asked to find. Before you read the text, work out what type of answer you are looking for.

1 If you are asked **when** something happened, you should look for a time or date.

> **1** According to Text A1, when should you check your tyres?

2 If you are asked **where** something happened, you should look for a place.

> **2** According to Text A1, where should you check your tyre pressure?

3 If you are asked **who** or **what** did something, you should look for a person or object.

> **3** What should you use to top up your washer fluid tank?

4 If you are asked **why** something happened, you should look for a reason.

> **4** Why should you ask someone to check your rear lights?

This student has underlined the key words and the type of answer they are looking for. They have found the correct answer by narrowing down their search and looking for a date.

Worked example

According to Text B2, <u>when</u> are the <u>new fitness classes</u> starting?

January

Now try this

Read Text A1 on page 50 and answer the question below.

Put a tick ✓ in the correct box.

According to Text A1, when do you need to ask someone to help you look after your car?

A when you check your tyres ☐

B when you check your oil ☐

C when you check your washer fluid levels ☐

D when you check your lights ☐

Using a dictionary

You will be asked to use a dictionary to find out the meaning of a word that appears in one of the texts.

Finding the page

The words in a dictionary are all listed in **alphabetical order**. To find a word in your dictionary you need to work through the following steps.

 Look at the first letter of the word you want to find. Think about where in the alphabet that letter appears. Find that section in the dictionary.

 When you have found the section containing all the words beginning with the first letter of your word, think about where the second letter of your word appears in the alphabet.

Finding the word

Your dictionary may have guide words at the top of each page.

- The word at the top of the left-hand page is the first entry on that page.
- The word at the top of the right-hand page is the last entry on that page.

These help you work out if you are on or near the right page for the word you are looking up.

Using a dictionary

The first letter 'e' will appear near the beginning of the dictionary.

The second letter 'x' appears towards the end of the alphabet. It will be on one of the last pages in the 'e' section.

The word you are looking for will usually be bold. The dictionary entry will tell you what type of word it is, and what it means.

> Look up the word 'extend' in your dictionary and write down what it means.

EXTEND

extend verb
to make larger
extender noun
a person or thing that extends something
extension noun
a part that is added to something
extent noun
the area covered by something
exterior noun
the area covered by something

Getting it right

Practise using your dictionary now so that you can find things quickly in the test.

Now try this

1 Rewrite this list of five words in alphabetical order.

   animal   statue   movement   above   machine

2 Look up the following words in your dictionary and write down what they mean.
   (a) vine
   (b) budget
   (c) omit

Choosing an answer

Multiple choice questions ask you to select **one** answer from a list of **four** possible answers.

Reading carefully

Some multiple choice options may seem similar, or you may think that they are correct based on your own knowledge.

1 When you are answering a multiple choice question, you must read the question and all the options very carefully.

2 All your answers must use information from the text. Even if you know something about the topic, you will not get marks if you use information not in the texts provided.

Checking your answers

Always check your answers.

✓ Read all the possible answers.

✓ Look carefully at the text and work out which one of the possible answers is the correct one.

✓ Tick **only** the answer you think is correct.

Multiple choice questions

For multiple choice questions, you will be asked to select **one** correct answer from a choice of **four** options. Put a tick in the box next to the correct answer.

If you change your mind about the answer, don't worry.

1 Put a line through the wrong answer.

2 Mark your new answer with a tick.

Read all the options carefully. Both A and B look similar, but there is only one correct answer.

You may have an idea of what the speed limit is in towns and cities, but you must find the correct answer in Text A2.

Go to page 5 to revise finding details.

According to Text A2, what is the speed limit in built-up areas such as towns and cities?

A 30mph ☐

B 35mph ☐

C 40mph ☐

D 70mph ☐

Now try this

Read Text B1 on page 52 and answer the question below.

Put a tick ✓ in the correct box.

According to Text B1, someone applying for the job of receptionist at Westerby Leisure Centre should have:

A a food hygiene qualification ☐

B basic computer skills ☐

C an interest in health and fitness ☐

D a clean driving licence ☐

Writing your own answer

Some of the questions in the reading test will ask you to write the answer to show that you have read and understood the text.

Short response questions

In some questions in your reading test, you will see the following instruction.

> **Write your answer on the line below.**

This means you need to find the correct answer in the text and write it down.

Example short answer

Look at the following extract from Text B1 (full text on page 52) and a student's answer to the test-style question below it.

✓ The student has identified the key words in the question and in the text, which has helped them to focus their search for the answer.

✗ There is no need to waste time writing a complete sentence. You only need to include the key information required to answer the question.

✓ This is the correct answer. It gives all the information needed to answer the question.

Text B1

We are looking for a <u>receptionist</u> to meet and greet our customers. You will <u>need</u>:
- <u>good communication skills</u>
- <u>a friendly manner</u>
- a willingness to learn about the services we provide and to answer customers' questions
- basic computer skills…

Getting it right

You don't need to write complete sentences in the reading test. Focus on giving the relevant information.

Worked example

Write your answer on the lines below.
According to Text B1, list **two** things you <u>need</u> to be a <u>receptionist</u> at Westerby Leisure Centre.

To be a receptionist you need to have a friendly manner and good communication skills.

Now try this

Read Text A2 on page 51, then answer the question below.

> **Write your answer on the line below.**
> According to Text A2, what type of road has a speed limit of 30mph?

Check your answer to make sure you have:
- chosen the correct answer
- given all the information needed to answer the question fully and accurately.

8

Putting it into practice

You now know what to expect from the questions in the reading test. Prepare for your test by practising the following:

- reading and understanding questions
- skim reading texts
- underlining key information while you read
- answering multiple choice questions
- answering short response questions.

Text B2

Fitness Classes

We are starting some new fitness classes in January. Details of times are in the timetable below.

January timetable for fitness classes

	10am–11am	7pm–8pm	8pm–9pm
Monday	Fitness @ 60+	Aerobics	Circuit training
Wednesday	Fitness @ 60+	Aerobics	Circuit training
Friday	Fitness @ 60+	Aerobics	Circuit training
Saturday	Body Blitz	Boxing circuits	Yoga

Each class <u>costs</u> £7 or you can buy a pass to all our classes for a whole week for just £17.

Worked example

Read Text B2 and answer the question below.

Write your answer on the line below.

According to Text B2, <u>how much</u> does it <u>cost</u> to attend all the fitness classes at Westerby Leisure Centre for a week?

~~Each class costs £7.~~

It costs £17 for a week.

✓ The student has identified and underlined the key words 'how much' and 'cost'. The student knows that they are looking for an amount of money in the text, which helps to focus their search.

✗ Initially, the student did not read the question carefully enough. They selected a piece of information from the text that does not answer the question. Make sure your answer matches the question.

✓ The student checked their answer and realised their mistake. They crossed out the incorrect answer and identified the correct answer.

Now try this

Read Text B2 on page 53 and answer the question below.

Write your answer on the line below.
According to Text B2, when will some new fitness classes be starting at Westerby Leisure Centre?

....

Headings and sub-headings

Headings and sub-headings will help you to read and understand the texts in the test.

Headings

A heading is the word or phrase at the top of a text that tells you what it's about. They are usually bigger than the rest of the text and a different colour to make them stand out.

Sub-headings

Writers use sub-headings to organise information into smaller sections. Looking at sub-headings in the test will help you to find the information you need to answer questions quickly.

Text B2

This **heading** tells you that the text is about news at Westerby Leisure Centre.

Westerby Leisure Centre Newsletter – November

Gym

This **sub-heading** tells you that the section that follows is about gym news. If there was a question about the gym, you should look here to find the answer.

Now try this

Read Text B2 on page 53, then answer the question below.

Put a tick ✓ in the correct box.

In which section of the text would you find information about the improved facilities?

A   Gym ☐

B   School holidays ☐

C   Fitness classes ☐

D   January timetable for fitness classes ☐

Paragraphs and bullet points

Paragraphs and bullet points are used to organise information in a text. They make the text easier to read, and easier for you to find the correct answers to the questions in the test!

Paragraphs

Paragraphs are collections of sentences that contain related information within a text. Each paragraph in a text focuses on a different aspect of the topic.

Bullet points

Bullet points split information into small chunks. This makes the information clear and the text easy to read.

When to start a new paragraph

A new paragraph starts when a new topic or idea begins.

The first paragraph of Text B1 focuses on information about Westerby Leisure Centre. It tells you **where** it is and **what** you can do there.

The second paragraph of Text B1 is about the **skills and qualities** you need to be a successful receptionist at Westerby Leisure Centre.

The writer has used bullet points here to make a clear list of all the skills and qualities you would need for the job.

The final paragraph of Text B1 gives information about **how** to apply for the job of receptionist at Westerby Leisure Centre.

Text B1

Paragraph 1

Located in the very centre of Westerby, our busy leisure centre offers a 25-metre swimming pool, fully equipped gym and sports hall. There's also a café offering an extensive range of healthy snacks and drinks.

Paragraph 2

We are looking for a receptionist to meet and greet our customers. You will need:

- good communication skills
- a friendly manner
- a willingness to learn about the services we provide and to answer customers' questions
- basic computer skills
- ideally some experience of cash handling and administrative work.

Paragraph 3

For more details and an online application form, visit the Vacancies page on our website.

Now try this

1 Read Text A2 on page 51 and note down what each paragraph or section is about.

2 Answer the question below.

Put a tick ✓ in the correct box.

According to Text A2, what are speed limits?

A The speed you should drive at in heavy rain or snow. ☐

B The speed you should drive at in high winds. ☐

C The maximum speed at which you can drive. ☐

D A guideline to help you decide how fast to drive. ☐

Tables and timetables

Tables and timetables present detailed information to the reader as clearly as possible.

Tables

Tables make information easy to find by presenting it in **rows** and **columns**. Rows and columns have **labels** and **headings** to indicate where information is placed in the table.

Timetables

Timetables are tables containing events that are arranged in a particular order according to the time they take place, such as lesson or bus timetables.

Text B2

January timetable for fitness classes

	10am–11am	7pm–8pm	8pm–9pm
Monday	Fitness @ 60+	Aerobics	Circuit training
Wednesday	Fitness @ 60+	Aerobics	Circuit training
Friday	Fitness @ 60+	Aerobics	Circuit training
Saturday	Body Blitz	Boxing circuits	Yoga

Rows go from left to right.

Cells are the individual boxes that make up the rows and columns.

Columns go up and down.

Using rows and columns

To find information in a table, you need to work out which column and row it is in.

When is the **Body Blitz** class?

1. Skim the table and find the cell that contains the words **Body Blitz**.
2. Follow the row to the left to see the day it is held on.
3. Follow the column to the top to see the time it is held at.

✓ 10am–11am on Saturdays

Which class is on at 7pm–8pm on Wednesdays?

1. Look for the row labelled **Wednesday**.
2. Look at the column labelled **7pm–8pm**.
3. Find the cell in the table where the **Wednesday** row meets the **7pm–8pm** column.

✓ Aerobics

Now try this

Look at the January timetable for fitness classes above, then answer the question below.

Put a tick ✓ in the correct box.

Liam wants to go to a yoga class. When could he go to a yoga class at Westerby Leisure Centre?

A Wednesday 7pm–8pm ☐   **B** Saturday 8pm–9pm ☐

C Saturday 10am–11am ☐   **D** Friday 7pm–8pm ☐

Forms

A form is a document with blank spaces for information to be inserted.

What do forms include?

Forms, such as application forms, request information in **two** ways.

1 Some forms include a prompt and a space to add the relevant information.

2 Some forms include tick boxes.

Name: Irenka Funar
Address: 7 Beech Lane, Westerby, PT7 4AU

Please tick any of the departments you would like to hear from:
☐ menswear
✓ womenswear
☐ children's wear

Reading a form

In the test, you could be asked to find particular information in a form. Forms can contain:

- information that the reader has filled in, such as their name and address
- instructions that the reader needs to know when they are completing the form, such as 'Please tick one box.'

Getting it right

In the test, make sure you read all the information on the form carefully – not just the parts that have been filled in.

Questions about forms

Read Text C2 on page 55 and look at a student's answer to the test-style question on the right.

✓ The student has found the relevant part of the text to answer the question.

✓ The student has provided **all** of the information for the correct answer. '28 days' would have been incorrect.

Worked example

Write your answer on the line below.
How long should Irenka wait for her discount card to arrive?
up to 28 days

Now try this

Read Text C2 on page 55, then answer the following questions.

6 Put a tick ✓ in the correct box.

Irenka would like to hear about new products and special offers by:

A post ☐   **B** text ☐

C email ☐   **D** none of the above ☐

7 On what date did Irenka complete this form?

You must read the text carefully. There are two dates on the form.

13

Putting it into practice

In this section you have revised identifying and understanding:

- titles and headings
- paragraphs and bullets
- forms
- tables and timetables.

Look at the extract from Text C1 and the test-style question below and read a student's answer.

Text C1

These are just some of our amazing offers:

In the <u>womenswear</u> department	In the menswear department	In the children's department
A huge range of bikinis, tankinis and all-in-ones from £14.99	Super-comfy, super-tough beach sandals, just £5.99	Cartoon T-shirts in a range of colours, just £3.99
<u>Flip-flops</u> just £6.99, available in blue, cream, pink or purple	Polo shirts £4.99 each or three for £10	Shorts for 4–14-year-olds, just £4.99

The sale is on from 8 to 22 June.

For more details, visit us in-store, online, or call us on 0800 600 323

Worked example

Read Text C1 and answer the question below.
Write your answer on the line below.
According to Text C1, which colour(s) of women's <u>flip-flops</u> can you buy in the sale at Anderson's department store?

Blue, cream

✓ The student has identified and underlined the key word 'flip-flops' in the question. They have found the same key word in the first column of the table, so they are able to focus their reading.

✗ The student did not read the text carefully enough and has left out some relevant information. Flip-flops are also available in pink and purple.

Now try this

Read Text C1 on page 54, then answer the question below.

Write your answer on the line below.
According to Text C1, what kinds of children's T-shirt are available in the sale at Anderson's department store?

....

Your writing test

In your writing test, you will be asked to complete two writing tasks.

The writing tasks

You will have **45 minutes** to complete **two** writing tasks worth a total of **20 marks**. The first writing task is worth **12 marks**. The second writing task is worth **8 marks**.

This time may be split over two or more sessions.

1 Read the task and any information provided.

2 Produce a brief plan.

3 Write a detailed answer.

4 Check your work.

Good writing skills

To do well in your writing test you need to:

✓ write clearly

✓ use details

✓ present information in a logical order

✓ use correct grammar, spelling and punctuation

✓ use suitable language for your audience

✓ use a suitable type of text and layout for the purpose.

Types of text

You could be asked to write any of the following:

email

letter

instructions

report

advert

personal statement

Go to pages 24–29 for help on all of these different kinds of text.

Now try this

1 How many writing tasks will you be asked to complete in your writing test?

2 How many marks is each task worth?

3 How much time will you be given to complete both writing tasks?

Reading the question

Reading the question carefully is very important. You must make sure you know exactly what the task is asking you to do.

Key words and phrases

Focus on the key information in the first two sections of the instructions to understand what you are being asked to write.

1 The first section gives some background information on what you are writing about.

2 The second section tells you who you are writing for and what kind of text you are writing.

Task A1

- You have <u>organised an event</u> to <u>raise money for charity.</u>

- Write a <u>letter</u> to your <u>local newspaper</u>, asking them to <u>put an article about your event in the newspaper.</u>

Re-read Task A1 above. Is it asking you to write a letter or a newspaper article? Make sure you know before you start writing!

Re-read the question

Always read the question twice. It can be easy to make a mistake and do what you **think** the instructions are telling you to do rather than what they are **actually** telling you to do.

Things to look out for

Make sure you have underlined:

✓ what you are writing about

✓ the kind of text you are writing

✓ who you are writing to

✓ why you are writing.

Getting it right

If you do not understand any of the writing task instructions, ask your teacher. Your teacher is allowed to help you understand the instructions – but they are not allowed to give you any ideas you could include in your writing!

Now try this

Look at the first two sections of Task A2 on the right. Write down your answers to the following questions.

1 What are you writing about?

2 What kind of text are you writing?

3 Who you are writing to?

4 Why you are writing?

Task A2

Your friend spends a lot of time on their mobile phone and laptop. You have planned an activity in your local area to get them away from their phone and laptop for a day.

Write an email to your friend, telling them about the activity you have planned.

Reasons for writing

It is important to think about the reason you are writing **before** you start planning or writing a text.

The purpose of the text

Before you start writing your response to a writing task, one of the first things you need to think about is the reason you are writing: the **purpose** of the text.

Look at this writing task. The purpose of the letter to the manager of the cinema is to:

- inform her about your skills and experience
- persuade her that you are the right person for the job.

Task C1

You see this poster pinned up in your local cinema.

Part-time staff wanted

Duties include:
- serving customers
- stocking the kiosk with sweets and drinks
- answering telephone calls
- cleaning.

To apply, write to the manager, Ms Anna Green.

Write a letter to Ms Green, applying for this job.

Thinking about your reader

Decide **what you want your reader to think** when they have read your writing. For example, it might be:

I think he's right. I should definitely follow the advice in this email.

This person has lots of experience of serving customers. I'm going to invite them for an interview.

✗ This student has not given enough thought to their reason for writing. The start of their letter does not aim to inform or persuade the manager.

Student A

Dear Ms Green

I really like going to the cinema so I'd love to do the job you advertised. One of my favourite films is ...

✓ This student has clearly thought about their reason for writing. Their letter informs the manager of the student's skills and experience, which will help to persuade the manager that they are the right person for the job.

Student B

Dear Ms Green

I am writing to apply for the part-time job. I have a lot of experience of serving customers as I used to ...

Now try this

Look at Task A1 on page 56.

1 What is the purpose of the letter it asks you to write?
2 What would you want the reader of the letter to think when they have read it?

Who you are writing to

When you write, you need to make sure your writing is suitable for its audience. The audience is the person who reads a text.

Who is your audience?

When you plan your answer to a writing task you need to think of ideas to include. Thinking about who the audience is can help you to come up with ideas, words and phrases that will make your writing more suitable for its audience.

Think about your reader. If the task asks you to write to a friend, you may find it helpful to have a real friend in mind as you write.

Write an email to your friend, giving them advice about which course to take.

If the task asks you to write to someone you do not know, it can be helpful to imagine them. Think about how you would talk to them if you met them in person.

Write a letter to Ms Green, applying for your dream job

Using informal language

If you are writing to someone you know, you can use **informal language**, for example:

- informal greetings, such as 'Hi'
- informal phrases, such as 'I aced it' instead of 'I completed it successfully'.

Hi Liam

I've done the test! I was a nervous wreck before it but I can't believe how well it went. I aced it!

Using formal language

If you are writing to someone you do not know, or to an official person or organisation, you should use **formal language**, for example:

- formal greetings, such as 'Dear'
- formal phrases, such as 'I completed it successfully' instead of 'I aced it'.

Dear Ms Okoye

I have recently taken a course in carpentry and joinery which I completed successfully.

Now try this

Look closely at Task B1 on page 58.

1 Think about the person you are writing to. What would they want or need to know? Note down some ideas.

2 What kind of language should you use? Note down some examples.

You recently bought a tea set online but when it arrived it was damaged.

Write a letter complaining to the company that you bought the item from.

Planning

Before you start writing, it is a good idea to make a plan.
You will receive marks for your plan for the first writing task.

Writing a good plan

Before you start planning, read the task and the information section carefully. Some tasks have bullet points that you can use as a starting point for your plan. In your plan you should include brief notes on:

• **who** you are writing to
• **why** you are writing to them
• any other **key information** you want to include.

Different types of plan

There are many different ways to plan your writing. Choose the method that suits you best.

Example

Look at this student's plan for Task B1 on the right.

Plan

• bought a tea set on the internet for £19.99
• when it arrive it was damaged
• there were cracks and sharp edges on the cups and saucers
• would like a refund

Task B1

You recently bought a tea set online but when it arrived it was damaged.

Write a letter complaining to the company that you bought the item from.

You could include:
• details of the item that you bought
• why you are unhappy with the item
• anything else you think the company needs to know
• what you would like the company to do.

Planning ideas

Ask yourself some questions to help you make planning notes.

When did I buy it? Last week.

Where did I buy it? From your website.

What is wrong with it? The cups and saucers are cracked.

How do I feel? Disappointed and upset.

Check your plan against the bullet points in the task. Have you covered them all?

Now try this

1 Look at Task B2 on page 59.
2 Write down some ideas you could include in your response.

Remember to:
• use the bullet points in the task to help you
• ask yourself some questions to come up with even more good ideas
• check you have covered all the bullet points in your plan.

Organising

When you have planned your ideas for the writing task, you need to organise them **before** you start writing.

Putting your ideas in order

In your writing test, you should write your ideas and points in **order of importance**. This will help your reader to follow your writing and understand the key information.

To avoid having to cross out your work, you should decide on the order of the ideas in your planning. Number your ideas in a **logical order** to help you.

> Go to page 19 to revise planning.

Go to page 19 to revise planning.

Planning tips

✔ Look carefully at your finished plan and the order in which you have numbered your ideas.

✔ Change your plan if you think you can improve it.

✗ Don't be afraid to reject an idea that doesn't seem to fit. If it doesn't work or fit in, it's better to leave it out.

✗ Don't rush into writing: it's much better to make improvements to your plan than to realise your writing isn't working when you're halfway through it!

Organising a plan

Look at this student's plan for a response to Task B1.

The student has numbered the ideas in a logical order. The student can turn this plan into a successful piece of writing by using the ideas in that order.

> You recently bought a tea set online but when it arrived it was damaged.
>
> Write a letter complaining to the company that you bought the item from.

<u>Plan</u>
- I bought a tea set for £19.99 ①
- It was broken when it arrived ④
- There were cracks and sharp edges on the cups and saucers ⑤
- I would like a refund ⑥
- I bought it last week ②
- I bought it from your website ③
- I feel disappointed and upset. ⑦

Put a tick next to each of the points in your plan when you have included it to make sure you have covered everything.

Now try this

1 Look carefully at Task C1 on page 60.
2 Write down some ideas you could include in your response.
3 Number all the ideas you have planned in a logical order.

Remember to check your plan carefully – and change it if you need to.

Drafting

In the first task of your writing test, you will be marked on your ability to plan and draft your writing before you write your final response.

Why is drafting important?

You should use your draft to:

- decide how you are going to order your ideas
- organise your ideas in paragraphs
- think about any details you might want to add to your writing.

Example draft

Write your draft in full sentences, not as notes. This will give you a much clearer idea of whether your final response will be successful.

Look at this student's plan and draft for Task B1 on the right.

> Go to page 19 to revise planning.

A new word has been added to the draft, making the writing more detailed.

The student has used this symbol to show that they will start a new paragraph here in their final response.

The student has included this final point, adding more detail to their letter.

Task B1

Write your plan and draft here:

Plan

- I bought a tea set for £19.99 ①
- It was broken when it arrived ④
- There were cracks and sharp edges on the cups and saucers ⑤
- I would like a refund ⑥
- I bought it last week ②
- I bought it from your website ③
- I feel disappointed and upset. ⑦

DRAFT

Dear Sir or Madam

I bought a tea set from your website last week for £19.99. It was badly broken when it arrived. The ^(broken) edges are really sharp and could have hurt someone. // I would like a refund because I feel disappointed and upset. ← that I wasted my money.

Yours faithfully

Alana Breck

Now try this

1 Plan and draft your response to Task A1 on page 56.
2 When you have completed your draft, check it carefully.

Task A1

You have organised an event to raise money for charity.

Write a letter to your local newspaper, asking them to put an article about your event in the newspaper.

Checking

It is important to leave time at the end of your writing tasks to check your work. Follow these steps to make sure you find any mistakes in your writing.

Careful checking

Always check your work carefully. It is a good idea to check it three times:

 once for spelling

 once for punctuation

 once to check it makes clear sense with no misused, repeated or missing words.

Checking for sense

When you check for sense, try to read aloud in your head. Imagine you can hear your voice. Does the work still make sense?

If you come across a sentence that doesn't make sense, read it again. Then think about what you can do to put it right.

Know your strengths

When you are preparing for your test and answering past test questions, you should identify which things you can do well and which things you find difficult. What kinds of mistake do you make:

- spelling mistakes
- missing or incorrect punctuation
- missing words
- using the wrong word?

Alarm bells

Train yourself to hear alarm bells when you come across tricky words, such as:

- their/there/they're
- its/it's
- your/you're.

Stop when you come to any of these words. Double check that you have used the correct spelling for the meaning you intended.

Putting it right

If you find a mistake – cross it out. Put ~~one neat line through the mistake~~ and add your correction:

- either by using an arrow (→) to the new words to guide the reader
- or by using an asterisk (*) *to tell the reader to read this bit next.

Getting it right

Remember to leave time to read through your work. Finish both writing tasks before checking, then go back to Task 1.

Leaving a brief break before checking your work will help to improve your focus.

Go to pages 46-48 to revise tricky spellings.

Now try this

Look at the draft you wrote in your response to the task on page 21. How many mistakes can you spot? Correct all the mistakes you can find.

Putting it into practice

You have now revised planning, drafting and checking.
Look at a student's response to Task B2 on page 59.

> Your friend wants to take a college course but cannot decide which one to do.
> Write an email to your friend, giving them advice about which course to take.

When you check your writing, check it at least three times, focusing on one thing at a time.

- **1st check:** look for sentences that do not make clear sense.
- **2nd check:** look for punctuation mistakes. Has every sentence got a capital letter at the start and a full stop at the end?
- **3rd check:** look for spelling mistakes. Keep an eye out for words that you know are tricky.

Hi Eva

I think you should do a course in
                    because
construction ~~becos~~ it would be realy
cool for a girl to be a builder. You
would lern lots things my friend jamie
done the same course and now he's
                          . He
learning bricklaying ~~he~~ really likes it.

Their are always lots of people who
need a builder so I think you could
           of
get lots ^ work when you have finished
~~the~~ the course. You could make lods of
money.

Love

Becca x

✓ corrected spelling
✓ full stop and capital letter added
✓ missed-out word added
✓ repeated word crossed out
✗ some incorrect spellings

> Go to pages
> 46-48 to revise
> tricky spellings.

Getting it right

Remember, you should only write key words and ideas in your plan. You should develop these main points in your draft and write in full sentences.

Now try this

1 Look again at the response above. Has the writer:
  - answered the question
  - planned and organised their ideas effectively, thinking about the person they are writing to
  - checked their writing carefully?
2 The student who wrote the response above has corrected some of their mistakes. Can you spot any more? Write out the response again, correcting the mistakes.
3 Plan and write your own response to Task B2.

Writing an email

In your writing test, you could be asked to write an email. You need to know how to write formal and informal emails.

How to begin an email

- If you **know the person** you are writing to, you can begin your email with the informal greeting 'Hi'.
- If you **do not know the person** you are writing to, or it is a more official email, you should begin your email with the formal greeting 'Dear...'

How to end an email

- If you **know the person** you are writing to, you could sign off informally with 'All the best' or 'Thanks'.
- If you **do not know the person** you are writing to, you should sign off more formally with 'Regards'.

Useful tips

In both formal and informal texts, you must do the following.

- Write in complete sentences.
- Use correct spelling, grammar and punctuation.
- Use paragraphs to put your points in a logical order.

You should avoid:

- text language, e.g. 'LOL'
- slang, e.g. 'I was gutted'
- contractions, e.g. 'I'm', 'don't'.

Informal email

Look at the example of an informal email on the right and the main features listed below.

- informal greeting
- informal phrases
- written in paragraphs
- abbreviations
- informal sign-off

Hi Ramesh,

I'm booking paintballing on Sat 2nd Aug, so you'd better be there and ready to rumble! It's me, you, Raj and Liam and it's going to be amazing.

I'll let you know if we need to take anything with us. Let me know if you can't make it.

All the best,

Adam

Formal email

Look at the example of a formal email on the right and the main features listed below.

- formal greeting
- complete words, not abbreviations
- written in paragraphs
- formal language
- formal sign-off

Dear Neil,

Further to our telephone conversation, I would like to book a day's paintballing session on Saturday 2nd August for four people.

Could you let me know if we need to bring anything with us and if lunch is included?

Thanks very much for your help.

Regards,

Adam

Now try this

Write a response to Task A2 on page 57.

Writing a letter

In your writing test, you could be asked to write a letter.

Features of a letter

If you are asked you write a letter in the test, you must include:

- the date on the right
- a greeting on the left
- formal language
- a new paragraph for each new point you want to write about
- a sign-off followed by your name.

> When you're writing a letter in real life, you would also need to include:
> - your address at the top right of the letter
> - the address of the person you are writing to lower down on the left.
>
> You don't need to write the addresses in the test.

17 Elm Drive
Westerby
PT9 4AQ

Ms Green
Westerby Picture Palace
Station Road
Westerby
PT3 7GT

18 March 2017

Dear Ms Green

I am writing to apply for the job which I saw in your...

〰〰〰〰〰〰〰〰〰〰〰〰〰〰

Yours sincerely,
Seph Reade

How to begin a letter

A letter always begins with 'Dear...', but there are **two** possibilities for what follows.

- If you know the name of the person you are writing to, you should write 'Dear Ms Green'.
- If you don't know the name of the person you are writing to, you should write 'Dear Sir or Madam'.

How to end a letter

A letter always ends with a formal sign-off.

- If you know the name of the person you are writing to, it should end with 'Yours sincerely'.
- If you don't know the name of the person you are writing to, it should end with 'Yours faithfully'.

Now try this

Write your response to Task B1 on page 58.

> Remember to:
> - use the correct layout
> - use an appropriate greeting and sign-off
> - use appropriate language, punctuation and grammar.

Writing instructions

In the test, you could be asked to write instructions to tell the reader how to do something. Instructions can take many different forms, including recipes, manuals and directions.

- Recipes instruct the reader how to prepare a meal.
- Manuals instruct the reader how to make or use something.
- Directions instruct the reader how to get from A to B.

A logical order

It is important to write the steps in instructions in the **correct order**. This will make it easier for the reader to follow.

 Put them in a **numbered list**:

1. Cut two slices of bread.
2. Butter both slices on one side.

 Signal the order using **words that indicate time**:

First cut two slices of bread then butter each slice on one side. **Next**, take...

You should decide the appropriate order of instructions in your plan so that your writing is logical.

Short steps

Instructions should be short and to the point so that the reader can follow them easily.

Instructions should contain an introduction that explains what the reader will need and what they will need to do.

When writing instructions, you should include just enough information for the reader to carry out the task. You should avoid including too many extra details.

Clear language

Begin each instruction with a **command verb**, telling the reader what to do. For example:

> **Boil** for 10 minutes.
> **Heat** the oven to 180°C.

Use language that the reader will understand. You should aim to use simple terms that most people will know and avoid using jargon.

Useful tips

Imagine yourself completing the task, thinking about each step you have to go through. Write the instructions in a logical order, remembering to use:

✓ clear language

✓ concise sentences

✓ command verbs

✓ numbered lists or time indicators.

Now try this

Complete the writing task below.

Write a set of instructions for a task you know how to do. It could be:

- a simple recipe, e.g. making a snack or a dessert
- using a gadget, e.g. sending a text or posting a photo on social media
- a practical task, e.g. changing a car tyre or putting on make-up
- something else.

Writing a report

Reports are formal texts that give the reader information about something they are interested in and would like to know more about.

When you write a report, remember to:

✓ use formal language: no slang or abbreviations

✓ write clear, complete sentences

✓ split it into paragraphs

✓ use correct grammar and punctuation.

Getting it right

When you have finished writing your report, read it back to yourself to make sure it is interesting and easy to follow.

Include an introduction

The first sentence or two of a report tells the reader what the report is about.

The introduction comes **after** the heading and **before** your sub-headings.

This report is about the food that is available in our college at the moment. It also suggests what could be done to make the food healthier.

Bullet point lists

Bullet points help to break up large amounts of text into small sections making information easier to read and understand.

At the moment, the canteen sells:
• a choice of hot meals including vegetarian options
• sandwiches
• crisps and snacks
• hot and cold drinks.

Now try this

Look at the writing task below. Write a plan for your response to this task.

Your school/college/workplace is asking for suggestions on how it could improve its appearance and become a more comfortable, attractive place to be and to work.

You have been asked to write a report on its appearance at the moment and make suggestions about how to improve it.

You could include:
• the appearance of the workspaces, open areas and corridors inside your building
• the outside of your building and the grounds
• how you think they could be improved.

Writing a notice or advert

A notice or advert needs to grab the reader's attention and give them information about the item or event it is advertising.

Give your notice a heading

You want people to read your notice or advert, so your heading needs to grab their attention. It should:

- give the reader information
- give a really positive impression of the item or event you are advertising.

Look at the headings on the right. A student considered using each one on a notice to advertise a sponsored walk. The walk was being organised to raise money for a local charity.

> Sponsored walk

This gives some information but is not very appealing.

> Brilliant family fun!

This sounds appealing but does not give the reader much information.

> Sponsored charity walk – fun for all the family!

This provides information and makes the event sound appealing.

Key information

In your notice or advert, you need to include everything a reader might need or want to know.

If it's an event, you need to tell readers:

- What it is
- When it is
- Where it is
- Why they should go
- How they can join in

If it's an item you are selling, you need to tell readers:

- What it is
- Why they should buy it
- How much it is

The Big Fun Swim for Guide Dogs

There will be a charity swim at Westerby Leisure Centre on 19th September at 2pm.

Join in and help raise money to train guide dogs for blind people. Ask your family and friends to sponsor you and you could make a really big difference to a blind person's life.

You can get a sponsor form from the leisure centre.

For more information, contact Richard Jones on 07740 60056

Now try this

Look at Task C2 on page 61.

Write your response.

> You have decided to sell something that you no longer need, using an online auction site.
> Write a notice giving details of the item.

Writing a personal statement

A personal statement is a summary of your skills and experience that you can send to a college or an employer.

The big questions

When you apply for a college course or a job, the big questions you need to answer are:

> Why am I interested?

> Why am I the right person?

A personal statement

The personal statement on the right was written as part of an application for a college course in carpentry and joinery.

In one section of your personal statement you should explain why you want to apply. Have you always been interested in this area? Has someone in this area inspired you?

You can then go on to give the reader information that shows why your skills and experience make you the perfect person for the college place or the job you are applying for.

Personal Statement

I have always been interested in making things out of wood and have had some tools of my own since I was twelve. I made my little sister a dolls' house when I was only fourteen and have wanted to be a carpenter and joiner ever since.

I have done work experience with a local carpenter every summer holiday for the last three years and have learned a lot from it. I will be taking my Design Technology GCSE in June. It is my favourite subject at school because I love making things.

Personal statement format

A personal statement usually includes very similar ideas and information to a letter. However, a personal statement does **not** have the same format as a letter. There is no need to include addresses, a greeting (Dear...) or a sign-off (Yours sincerely...). You **do** need to write in paragraphs.

Golden rule

A personal statement is a formal text so you should:

✓ write in paragraphs

✓ write in complete sentences

✓ use formal language: no slang or abbreviations

✓ use correct punctuation and grammar.

Now try this

Look at the job description from Task C1 on page 60. Write a personal statement that you could use in your application for this job.

You see this poster pinned up in your local cinema:

Part-time staff wanted

Duties include:

- serving customers
- stocking the kiosk with sweets and drinks
- answering telephone calls
- cleaning.

Putting it into practice

Make sure you know the different features of letters, emails, instructions, reports, notices and personal statements. They will help you structure and express your ideas in your responses in the writing test.

Look at two students' responses to the tasks below.

Task B1

You recently bought a tea set online but when you arrived it was damaged.

Write a letter complaining to the company that you bought the item from.

Task B2

Your friend wants to take a college course but cannot decide which one to do.

Write an email to your friend, giving them advice about which course to take.

> 17 Acorn Lane
> Minchester
>
> Dear Sir or Madam
>
> I bought a tea set from you the other day and I'm not happy with it. It's really rubbish, the cups and saucers are totally smashed up. I'm gutted.
>
> I'm going to send the tea set back and I want a refund please.
>
> Best wishes
>
> Naz

✗ The date is missing.

✗ The language used is too informal.

> Dear Billy
>
> I heard you want to do a college course but can't decide which one. I think you should do one with cars because you've always loved cars. You'd be a great mechanic and you can help me get my car sorted when I buy it.
>
> I hope you listen to my advice.
>
> Yours sincerely
>
> Jamie

✓ Email layout is correct.

✗ Some of the language used is too formal for an email to a friend.

Now try this

1 Note down all the errors you can find in the two responses above. Think about:
   - what is missing in the layout
   - language that is too formal or informal.
2 Rewrite both these responses, making sure you:
   - use the correct layout
   - use appropriately formal or informal language.

Paragraphs

In both of your writing tasks you need to structure your writing in paragraphs.

Using paragraphs

A paragraph is a chunk of writing that focuses on one aspect of a topic or subject.

Each time you start writing about a different aspect of your topic, you need to start a new paragraph.

You can use the bullet points in the task to help you organise your ideas into paragraphs.

How long is a paragraph?

A paragraph is usually made up of more than one sentence. There are **no rules** about how long a paragraph can or should be. Start a new paragraph when you change topic or change your focus to a new aspect of the same topic.

Setting out paragraphs

When you write **by hand**, you do not usually leave a line blank between paragraphs. You start your paragraph on a new line and indent your writing – this means leaving a small space at the beginning of the first line of your paragraph.

When you type on a **computer**, you can start a new paragraph by leaving a line blank and starting your new paragraph on the next line.

Task A1

Write a letter to your local newspaper, asking them to put an article about your event in the newspaper.

You could include:

- why you are writing
- details of the event you have planned
- the charity you are raising money for
- why you think local people will enjoy the event.

Each of the paragraphs in this letter focuses on a different aspect of the topic.

Sample answer

Dear Sir or Madam

I am writing to ask if you would put an article in your paper about the charity event that I am organising.

The event is a sponsored walk which we will be doing on 3rd October. We are asking people to walk ten miles round the park; that's ten laps of the park.

We are going to raise money for the NSPCC, which I think is a really good charity. They help children who are in trouble so it would be great if we could raise as much money as possible.

I think people round here would love to help, so please help us let them know about it in an article in the paper.

Yours faithfully

Now try this

Look at Task B1 on page 58.

1. Plan your response to Task B1, noting all the ideas you will include.
2. Mark on your plan where you will start a new paragraph. You could do this by drawing a line across your plan and labelling it 'NP' (New Paragraph).

Sentences

In each of your writing tasks, you should write in complete sentences.

What is a sentence?

A sentence tells the reader at least one piece of information or idea.

A sentence contains at least one verb. A verb is a word that describes the following:

- **actions, e.g.** He rides his bike to the shops.
- **incidents, e.g.** He fell off his bike.
- **situations, e.g.** He was badly hurt.

 Each of these is a complete sentence that makes sense by itself.

Punctuating sentences

Every sentence you write should begin with a capital letter and end with one of the following:

- full stop
- question mark
- exclamation mark.

 Punctuation helps the reader know when a sentence starts and finishes, making a text easier to understand.

This version is missing a full stop and capital letter. It is confusing to read and difficult to understand.

> We will have a great time when you get home you'll be glad you made the effort.

This version has a full stop and capital letter in the correct places, making it much clearer and easier to read.

> We will have a great time. When you get home, you'll be glad you made the effort.

Adding detail to sentences

You can make your sentences clearer and more interesting by adding detail to them. One way to do this is with **adjectives** and **adverbs** – words that add description and detail to nouns and verbs.

The meaning of these sentences is clear, but they could be more interesting and more detailed.

> Don't spend the day staring at your phone. Come and have some fun!

These sentences are much more interesting!

> Don't spend the <u>entire</u> day staring <u>pointlessly</u> at your phone. Come and have some <u>serious</u> fun!

Now try this

Look at some notes that one student made in response to Task C1 on page 60.

1 Rewrite the notes on the right as complete sentences.

2 Check that you have begun each sentence with a capital letter and finished it with a full stop.

3 Does each sentence you have written make sense?

- weekend work at supermarket for 2 years
- experience of serving customers
- unloading deliveries
- stocking shelves

Talking about the present

You need to know how to use the present tense to write about things that are happening now.

Verbs

The verb in a sentence tells the reader whether something is happening now, in the past, or in the future.

> I <u>work</u> in a local garage.

This verb is in the present tense. It tells the reader that this is the current situation.

The present tense

The present tense can be used to express:

- something that is happening now:
  I am eating a sandwich.
- the situation at the moment:
  I live in the United Kingdom.

- something that happens over and over again:
  I go to college one day a week.
  I play netball every Tuesday evening.

Using the present tense

There are two ways of using the present tense.

In this one, you use just the main verb.

Are you at school?
No, I <u>go</u> to college.

2 In this one you add 'am', 'is' or 'are' before the verb, and you add '-ing' to the verb.

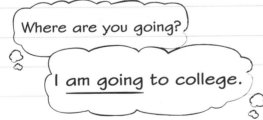
Where are you going?
I <u>am going</u> to college.

Who is doing the verb?

In the present tense, the verb can change depending on who is doing the action the verb describes.

I	go	to college.
You	go	to college.
He/She/It	goes	to college.
We	go	to college.
They	go	to college.

Notice how the verb for 'he', 'she' and 'it' is different from all the others. You always add '-s' or '-es' to the verb for these.

In this form of the present tense, it is this verb that changes depending on who is doing the action the verb describes.

I	am	going	to college.
You	are	going	to college.
He/She/It	is	going	to college.
We	are	going	to college.
They	are	going	to college.

Now try this

Look at the extract on the right from a student's response to Task B2 on page 59.
Rewrite each sentence in the present tense.

You loved going on holiday. You were always good at finding interesting places to visit. I thought a course in travel and leisure was perfect for you.

33

Making the verb match

Verbs change their form depending on their subject. You need to check that you have used the right form of verb in every sentence of your writing.

Subject and verb

Most sentences have a subject and a verb. The subject is whoever or whatever is doing the thing that the verb describes.

<u>Jamie painted</u> the wall

'Jamie' is the subject of the verb 'painted'. Jamie is doing the painting.

<u>He painted</u> the wall.

'He' is the subject of the verb 'painted'. He is doing the painting.

<u>The wall collapsed</u>.

'The wall' is the subject of the verb 'collapsed'. The wall is doing the collapsing.

Making the verb match

To make the verb match the subject, you need to choose the right form of the verb. Most verbs have only two forms in the present tense:

* go / goes
* do / does
* drive / drives
* live / lives

You add '-s' or '-es' when a 'he', a 'she' or an 'it' is doing the verb:

✓ I <u>drive</u> my car to work every morning.

✓ He <u>drives</u> his car to work every morning.

Singular or plural?

Working out whether the subject is singular or plural can help you choose the correct verb form.

* If there is only one of something, we use a singular noun, e.g. 'a man'.
* If there are more than one of something, we use a plural noun, e.g. 'two men'.

You add '-s' or '-es' when the subject is a singular noun:

✓ One man runs for the bus.

✓ Two men run for the bus.

To be

One very common verb is the verb 'to be'. It has three different forms in the present tense:

I	am
you	are
he/she/it	is
we	are
they	are

You will definitely use this verb in your writing tasks. Make sure you choose the correct form when you do!

Now try this

Look closely at the subjects and verbs in the sentences on the right.

1 Underline the verbs and the subjects in each sentence.
2 Circle any verbs that are incorrect.
3 Rewrite the sentences using the correct verb forms.

A I love playing football for my local team.

B We was first in our league last season.

C Our manager train us every week and we work hard for him.

D The whole team love him.

Talking about the past

To write about things that have already happened you will need to use the past tense.

Verbs

It is the verb in a sentence that tells the reader that something is happening in the past.

> I did a month's work experience at a local garage.

This sentence is in the past tense. It is about something that has already happened. The verb 'did' signals this.

Verbs with their own rules

Some verbs have an unusual past tense. Make sure you know these ones:

I go	> I went	I make	> I made
I do	> I did	I come	> I came
I see	> I saw	I find	> I found
I eat	> I ate	I know	> I knew
I get	> I got	I buy	> I bought
I take	> I took	I bring	> I brought

Putting the verb in the past

To put a verb into the past tense, you often add '-ed':

I play the guitar.   I played the guitar.

If the verb ends in '-e', you often just add '-d':

I like cooking.   I liked cooking.

Sometimes you double the last letter of the verb and add '-ed':

I stop quickly.   I stopped quickly.

If the verb ends in '-y', you change the '-y' to '-ied':

I hurry to work.   I hurried to work.

I apply for a job.   I applied for a job.

To be

One of the trickiest verbs in the past tense is the verb 'to be'. It's a verb you will need to use often in your writing, so make sure you know how to use it correctly. Remember the different forms it has in the past and the present tense.

present tense	past tense
I am	I was
You are	You were
He/She/It is	He/She/It was
We are	We were
They are	They were

Be careful! It's very easy to get 'was' and 'were' mixed up.

Now try this

The student answer below is all in the present tense.
1 Rewrite the sentences, putting them in the past tense.
2 Check they still make sense.

> I try my best in my job. I work hard. I never stop trying and I always find solutions to problems. My ambition is to become a manager.

35

Talking about the future

You may want to talk about the future in your writing. For example, in a job application you might want to write about what you think or hope will happen in the future.

Using 'will'

One way we talk about the future is using the verb 'will'.

The verb 'will' never changes to match the subject.

Go to pages 34 and 35 for more help on the verb 'to be'.

now	in the future
I am at college.	I <u>will</u> leave at the end of the year.
I live in London.	Soon I <u>will</u> move to Scotland.

Using 'going to'

We also use the verb 'going to' to talk about the future.

The verb 'to be going to' changes to match the subject.
<u>I am</u> going to call you.
<u>You are</u> going to call me.
<u>He/She/It</u> is going to call me.
<u>We are</u> going to call you.
<u>They are</u> going to call you.

now	in the future
I am at college.	I <u>am going</u> to leave at the end of the year.
I live in London.	Soon I <u>am going</u> to move to Scotland.

The immediate future

If something is happening very soon, we use the phrase 'about to':

I am <u>about to</u> start a new course in bricklaying.

He is <u>about to</u> go to Australia.

We are <u>about to</u> go to the cinema.

Possible futures

Sometimes you will want to write about things that could possibly happen in the future. To do this we use verbs to express how likely or possible we think these are:

I <u>would like</u> to be an astronaut.

I <u>hope to</u> become a mechanic.

I <u>might</u> buy a car.

I <u>may</u> buy a bicycle.

Now try this

The student answer below is all in the present tense.
1 Rewrite the sentences using the future tense.
2 Read through your answers to check that:
   • you have put all the sentences into the future
   • the sentences all make clear sense

I try my best in my job. I work hard. I never stop trying and I always find solutions to problems. My ambition is to become a manager.

Using joining words

The instructions in your writing test will ask you to write complete sentences using joining words (conjunctions) like *and*, *as*, *but* and *or*.

Linking ideas

You can use joining words to link ideas.

This makes your meaning clearer. For example:

I love cooking. I usually make dinner for my family.

I love cooking <u>and</u> I usually make dinner for my family.

This joining word shows that the two parts of the sentence are connected.

I love cooking. I hate washing up.

I love cooking <u>but</u> I hate washing up.

This joining word shows that the second part of the sentence contrasts with the first part.

Adding details

You can use joining words to add detail to your writing and make your sentences more interesting.

Ask yourself:

When?

| I love shopping | when | I have some money. |
| | until | I run out of money. |

Why not?

I love cooking	unless	I'm too busy.
	but	I hate washing up.
	although	I am not very good at it.

Why?

I have a part-time job	as	I want to get more experience.
	so	I can support myself.
	because	I go to college three days a week.

Now try this

Write 5–10 sentences on a subject you know a lot about.

Use a different one of these joining words in each of your sentences. You could tick each one off as you use it.

and	if
but	because
or	as
so	although
when	until

Putting it into practice

You have now revised:

- writing in paragraphs and sentences
- writing about the past
- writing about the present
- writing about the future.

Look at a student's response to Task A1.

19 May 2017

Dear Sir or Madam

We are organising a sponsored run for charity.

We run three miles and raise lots of money.

We was hoping that you could put an article in your newspaper. People would hear about the run. More people would want to join in.

We done the same thing last year. We made more than a thousand pounds. We want to make even more this year. Please help us.

Yours faithfully

This is an effective opening sentence, but it could be more detailed:

- Why are you organising a run for charity?
- Which charity will you give the money to?
- How could you link these details using joining words?

The writer has not checked this sentence. It is about the future but it uses the present tense.

Some of these ideas could be clearer if the writer used joining words to link them.

Some of these sentences could be linked using joining words.

There are some mistakes in the writer's sentences, which can create the wrong impression. It can seem rude or careless to send a letter that is full of mistakes.

Now try this

Rewrite the letter above, aiming to:

- add more detail using joining words
- link some ideas using joining words
- check that every sentence uses the correct tense
- check that every sentence uses the correct verb form.

Capital letters

You must use capital letters correctly in both your writing tasks.

At the start of a sentence

The first word in a new sentence always begins with a capital letter.

We went to the cinema. The film was fantastic.

The full stop marks the end of the sentence.

When talking about yourself

Whenever you talk about yourself, the word 'I' must always be a capital letter.

It is a sunny day so I will go to the beach.

You will lose marks if you use the lowercase 'i' when talking about yourself.

For people's names

People's names always begin with a capital letter.

Hi Emily

Dear Ms Green

This rule includes the word 'Sir' or 'Madam' at the beginning of a letter.

Dear Sir or Madam

It's the name you are using for the person you are writing to!

Other uses

You also need to use a capital letter for the following.

- **Titles** Star Wars is my favourite film ever.
- **Places** I was born in Manchester.
- **Companies** I have worked at Jane's Hair Salon for three years.
- **Languages** I can speak English, French and Spanish.
- **Special occasions** Christmas, Diwali, Ramadan
- **Days of the week** Monday, Friday, Sunday
- **Months of the year** January, June, December

Now try this

Rewrite the letter below, adding capital letters where necessary.

75 long lane
missleford
rb7 6rr
5th january 2017

dear ms green

i am writing to apply for the job at westerby picture palace. i have lots of experience of stocking shelves and serving customers as i have been working at westerby petrol station for the past two months. it would be great to work in a cinema because i love films.

yours sincerely
aran white

Ending a sentence

A sentence is not complete unless it ends with the correct punctuation mark. Writing in complete sentences is really important in your writing test.

Full stops

The full stop is probably the most important punctuation mark, so it is important that you remember to use full stops – and use them correctly.

One common and very easy mistake to make is to use a comma when you should use a full stop.

✗ Sarah loves to dance, she competes in the local competition.

✓ Sarah loves to dance. She competes in the local competition.

When to use full stops

A full stop marks the end of each piece of information.

✓ I bought a mobile phone from you last week. It does not work.

A joining word links two ideas.

✓ I bought a mobile phone from you last week but it does not work.

Go to page 37 to revise joining words.

Question marks

A question should always end with a question mark.

You can usually recognise a question for one of the reasons below:

• it is a sentence that is asking for a reply
• it begins with one of the question words 'Who', 'What', 'Where', 'Why', 'When' or 'How'
• the verb comes before the subject, for example:

Has she been to London?

verb   subject

Do you think you'll get the job?

Exclamation marks

Exclamation marks are rarely used in formal texts.

You might use one in a less formal email to a friend:

✓ It would be amazing if you could come out with me on Tuesday!

You are unlikely to use an exclamation mark in a formal letter like a job application:

✗ I am applying for this job because I have lots of experience in this area!

The golden rule of exclamation marks: if you are in any doubt, don't use them.

Now try this

Rewrite the student text on the right, adding the correct punctuation.

I bought a mobile phone from you last week it does not work I cannot get a signal anywhere it will not connect to wi-fi would you please let me know how I can get a refund thank you

40

Putting it into practice

You have now revised the correct use of full stops and capital letters.

Look at a student's response to Task B1 on page 58.

74 Lime Walk
Newcastle
NE72 5QR

✓ Capital letters used correctly.

✗ Some capital letters are missing here.

✓ Full stops used accurately.

electricals R Us
7 London Road
NT6 5RT

19 may 2017

Dear sir or madam

I bought a tea set from your website
and when it arrived it was broken.

• The saucers are chipped.
• There are sharp edges on the cups.
• The tea pot doesn't pour properly.

I want to change it for a new one
please, could you tell me where I
should send it

✗ The comma in this sentence should be replaced with a full stop or a joining word.

✗ Full stop is missing here

✗ Capital letter missing here.

yours faithfully

Chantelle Grundy

Now try this

Rewrite the response above, correcting any instances where capital letters or full stops have been missed.

Spelling tips

You should check any spellings you are unsure about in your writing test. You will have a dictionary – but looking words up in the dictionary takes time. Revise these spelling tips to help you check your spelling more quickly.

Sound it out and look

If you are unsure about a spelling, imagine hearing it aloud inside your head. Focus on each syllable and try to picture the word written down on paper.

✓ fantastic

Try spelling it two or three different ways on a scrap of paper. Which one *looks* correct?

Silent letters

Words with silent letters are some of the trickiest spellings because you can't sound them out.

- Think about all the question words that begin with **wh**:

  when   which   who   where   why

- Think about words that sound like they begin with **n** but actually begin with a silent **k**:

  knee   knife   knock   know

- Think about words with a silent **b**:

  thumb   bomb   climb   crumb   doubt

- Think about words with a silent **l**:

  could   would   should   half   talk   walk

Double letters

Words with double letters can be difficult to spell. If you say the word out loud, you can't hear whether it should be a double letter or a single letter. Learn how to spell these words saying each syllable out loud so that you hear both the double letters:

address   different   tomorrow
skills   possible   success

-ly or -ley?

When you add **ly** to a word that ends in **e**, make sure you don't swap the **l** and the **e**:

✗ sincerley   ✓ sincerely
✗ safley   ✓ safely
✗ rudley   ✓ rudely

Very few words end in **ley**, for example: alley, barley, valley, trolley.

Now try this

Make a list of all the words on this page which you do not feel confident about spelling.

1 Look at the word on this page.
2 Say the word out loud.
3 Cover the word.
4 Write the word down on paper.
5 Uncover the word and check your spelling.
6 Repeat until you are absolutely sure you know how to spell the word.

Plurals

A plural is the form of a word that shows you are talking about more than one. For example, **books** is the plural of **book**. The spellings of some plurals can be tricky.

Adding s

The plural of most words is formed simply by adding **s** to the end of the word.

one house	two houses
one job	two jobs
one time	two times
one pencil	two pencils

Adding es

If a word ends in **ch**, **sh**, **x**, **s** or **ss**, you add **es** to form the plural. Read this list of examples aloud and listen carefully. Say the plural aloud and listen to see whether you need an extra **e** to create the plural.

one lunch	two lunches
one wish	two wishes
one box	two boxes
one boss	two bosses

Words that end in y

If the letter before the final **y** is a vowel (a, e, i, o or u), add **s** to make the plural.

one day	two days
one boy	two boys
one key	two keys

If the letter before The **y** is a consonant (any letter that is not a vowel), the **y** becomes **ies**.

one party	two parties
one country	two countries
one family	two families

Words that don't follow the rules

Some words change much more in the plural:

one woman	two women
one man	two men
one foot	two feet
one child	two children
one mouse	two mice
one tooth	two teeth
one person	two people

And some don't change at all, for example:

one fish	two fish
one sheep	two sheep
one deer	two deer

Now try this

Write out the following sentences, choosing the correct spellings.

1 He trys/tries to put healthy lunchs/lunches in his children's lunchboxs/lunchboxes every day.

2 She sits on one of the benches/benchs in the park, eating her sandwichs/sandwiches.

3 I have happy memories/memorys of my journies/journeys to London.

Prefixes

A prefix is a letter or group of letters which you can add to the beginning of a word to create a new word with a different meaning.

Prefixes change meaning

When you add a prefix, you change the meaning of the word you are adding it to (the root word). The meaning of the new word is usually related to the meaning of the root word.

prefix		root word		new word
un		fair		unfair
dis	+	respect	=	disrespect
mis		spell		misspell
re		do		redo

Never change the spelling of the root word when you add a prefix.

The meaning of common prefixes

Learning the meaning of common prefixes will help you understand the meaning and spelling of words you don't know.

prefix	meaning
un-	not, e.g. unfriendly, unable
pre-	before, e.g. prefix, premature
co-	with, e.g. cooperation, co-pilot
extra-	beyond, e.g. extracurricular, extraordinary
re-	again, e.g. return, rewind

Opposites

A lot of prefixes are used to create opposites.

prefix		root word		opposite
un		kind		unkind
dis		appear		disappear
mis	+	trust	=	mistrust
in		visible		invisible
im		possible		impossible

The *al-* prefix

When the prefix 'all' is added, the second 'l' disappears and it becomes 'al-'.

prefix		root word		new word
		ready		already
all	+	ways	=	always
		together		altogether

Now try this

Make a list of all the words you can think of that begin with the prefixes:

- un
- mis.

Remember to check your spelling of the root word!

Some words that start with the letters 'un' and 'mis' aren't made up of a prefix and a root word, such as 'under' and 'mission'.

Suffixes

A suffix is a letter or group of letters which you can add to the end of a word to create a new word.

Suffixes change meaning

Adding a suffix to a root word can change its meaning. The spelling of the root word usually stays the same when you add a suffix.

root word		suffix		new word
play		ed		played
play		er		player
play		ing		playing
short	+	est	=	shortest
kind		ness		kindness
accident		al		accidental
accept		able		acceptable
enjoy		ment		enjoyment

Root words ending with a consonant

- When you add a suffix to most shorter root words that end with a single consonant, you double that final consonant:

  stop + ing = stopping

  grab + ed = grabbed

- If the root word ends with two consonants, you don't double the final consonant when you add a suffix:

  fast + er = faster

  try + ing = trying

Root words ending in y

- When you add most suffixes to a root word ending with a consonant + **y**, the **y** changes to an **i**:

  carry + ed = carried

  happy + ness = happiness

  beauty + ful = beautiful

- When you add the suffix **ing** to those words, the **y** doesn't change:

  carry + ing = carrying

Root words ending in e

- You usually (but not always) take the **e** off the end of a word when adding a suffix that begins with a vowel:

  write + ing = writing

- There are exceptions to this:

  excite + ment = excitement

Now try this

Make a list of all the words you can think of that end with the suffixes on this page. Make sure you follow the rules for the tricky spellings – then double-check your spelling using a dictionary or the internet.

Tricky spellings 1

You will need to use correct spellings for both writing tasks.

There, their, they're

Their means belonging to them:

Their football boots are muddy.

There is used to explain the position of something:

The football boots were over there.

Or to introduce a sentence:

There is a place for muddy boots outside.

They're is a contraction of **they are**:

They're all tired after the football game.

We're, wear, where and were

We're is a contraction of **we are**:

We're going to Spain.

Wear is a verb (doing word) that refers to clothing:

You need to wear a uniform at our school.

Were is the past tense of **are**:

They were late getting to the airport.

Where refers to place:

Where are we going?

Your, you're

Your means belonging to you.

You're is a contraction of **you are**.

✗ ~~Your~~ having the time of ~~you're~~ life

✓ You're having the time of your life.

To, too, two

To indicates place, direction or position:

I went to Spain.

Two is a number:

Two of us went to Spain last year.

Too means 'also', or a large amount:

I went too far.

Of, off

The easiest way to remember the difference is by listening to the sound of the word you want to use:

- **of** is pronounced 'ov'
- **off** rhymes with 'cough'

✗ He jumped ~~of~~ the top ~~off~~ the wall.

✓ He jumped off the top of the wall.

Getting it right

Make sure you know these common spelling errors. Check that you have used the correct word in your writing at the end of the test.

Now try this

Select the correct spelling in these sentences.
1 I found out <u>where/were</u> they <u>where/were</u> going.
2 <u>They're/there</u> going <u>they're/there</u> later.
3 Lots <u>of/off</u> people are heading <u>of/off</u> on holiday.
4 <u>They're/Their</u> not sure <u>where/were</u> they lost <u>they're/their</u> money.
5 I worked in a company <u>where/were</u> there <u>where/were</u> <u>alot/a lot</u> <u>of/off</u> other young people.

Tricky spellings 2

You will need to use the correct words for both writing tasks.

Would have, could have, should have

Students often use 'would of', 'could of' or 'should of' instead of **would have, could have** or **should have**. For example:

Accidents could of been prevented. We should of fixed the pavement as soon as the cracks appeared.

This student **should have** written: Accidents **could have** been prevented. We **should have** fixed the pavement as soon as the cracks appeared.

Bought or brought?

Bought and **brought** mean different things.

Bought is the past tense of **buy**:

Ravi bought an umbrella in the shop.

Brought is the past tense of **bring**:

Ravi brought an umbrella in her bag.

Are, our

Are is a verb (doing word):

We are going to the airport.

Our means belonging to us:

Our football boots are very muddy.

Write or right

Write and **right** mean different things.

Write means to put something in writing, using a pen or pencil:

I need to write a shopping list.

Right is the opposite of **wrong**:

I need to know the right spelling for difficult words.

Know, no and now

Know means to have knowledge:

I know enough to pass my test.

Now means at the present time:

I now know enough to pass my test.

No is the opposite of **yes**:

'No! That spelling is not correct!'

Now try this

Select the correct spellings in these sentences.
1 Two/too people brought/bought a cake to/too college.
2 I was too/to full too/to eat any.
3 Are/Our you going too/to eat some know/now?
4 I have got know/no idea if I brought/bought them home or left them behind.
5 I know/no what I should have/should of done.

Tricky spellings 3

You should practise spelling words correctly and build up your vocabulary before your writing test.

Learn correct spellings

Get into the habit of looking up new or unfamiliar words in a dictionary before your test. Then practise the correct spelling. You could use the look/cover/write/check method:

1 Look at the word.

2 Cover the word.

3 Write it from memory.

4 Check your spelling.

Say what you see

Say the word aloud, breaking it into smaller parts. For example, say these words aloud to help you with the correct spelling:

def / in / ite / ly

fri / end

Wed / nes / day

Find hidden words

For example, **separate** becomes much easier to spell if you remember there is 'a rat' inside it:

sep-**a-rat**-e

Go to page 6 for tips on how to use a dictionary.

Getting it right

If any of the words in this book unfamiliar, look them up in a dictionary. That way you will be building up your vocabulary for the test!

Now try this

Make a list of any words you have trouble spelling.

Think of a rhyme to help you to remember these tricky spellings.

Putting it into practice

You have revised lots of spelling tips and hints. Look at a student's response to Task B2 below.

Hi Marin

I heard you <u>wear</u> thinking of going to college and wanted to <u>no</u> what course to do. I think you <u>shud</u> do a course in retail <u>becos</u> you <u>wud</u> be brilliant at <u>runing</u> a shop. You are great at <u>chating</u> to <u>peeple</u>. <u>Their</u> are loads of <u>diffrent</u> kinds of shops. It's your <u>disicion</u>!

I <u>no</u> I <u>shud</u> <u>of</u> <u>thort</u> of this before but there hasn't been much time <u>becos</u> I've been <u>to</u> busy at college. I've been <u>rushd</u> <u>of</u> my feet. Sorry!

Best <u>wishs</u>

Gov

X The underlined words are all spelled incorrectly. Think about why the student has made these spelling mistakes – and how the words should be spelled.

The writer needs to think about:

- words with different meanings that sound the same but are spelt differently
- words with silent letters
- root words that change when you add a prefix
- the vowels in words that people often spell incorrectly
- plurals that are formed in different ways.

Checking spelling

When you are checking a piece of writing for spelling mistakes, try reading your writing backwards as well as forwards: from bottom to top and from right to left.

This stops you thinking about the meaning of the writing and helps you focus on the spelling.

Ask yourself:

> Which one looks wrong?

> Which one looks right?

Remember to experiment. Pick out the words you think may be wrong and try spelling them in two or three different ways.

Now try this

Rewrite the response above, making sure you correct all the underlined spelling mistakes.

Check your answer when you have finished. Make a note of all the spelling mistakes you did not spot or were not sure how to correct. Then go back to pages 46–48 and find the page that will help you learn them.

TEXT A1

Stacey reads the information sheet she was given when she bought a car.

How to Look After Your Car

EVERY WEEK:

Check your tyres

Make sure your tyres are not damaged and check the tyre pressure at a petrol station.

EVERY TWO WEEKS:

Check your oil

Use the dipstick to check you have enough oil. Top up the oil using the right grade of oil for your engine.

EVERY MONTH:

Check your washer fluid levels

Make sure the washer fluid tank is full. If it is not, top it up with water and screenwash.

Check your lights

Check all the lights on your car are working properly. Ask someone to help you check the rear lights.

TEXT A2

Stacey reads the following information on a website about how to drive safely.

www.estrickspeedlimits.com

Speed limits

The speed limit is the maximum speed at which you can drive. It may not always be safe to drive at that speed. In difficult driving conditions such as high winds, heavy rain or snow, you should reduce your speed.

These guidelines give information about the speed limit for cars, motorcycles and vans on different types of road.

Type of road	Speed limit in miles per hour	Speed limit in kilometres per hour
in built-up areas (towns and cities)	30	48
single carriageways	60	96
dual carriageways	70	112
motorways	70	112

If you do not see a sign showing the speed limit, the limit is 30 miles per hour (or 48 kilometres per hour).

Help   Contact Us   About Us

TEXT B1

Sam reads this poster in his local leisure centre.

RECEPTIONIST WANTED!

Westerby Leisure Centre

Located in the very centre of Westerby, our busy leisure centre offers a 25-metre swimming pool, fully equipped gym and sports hall. There's also a café offering an extensive range of healthy snacks and drinks.

We are looking for a receptionist to meet and greet our customers. You will need:

 good communication skills

 a friendly manner

 a willingness to learn about the services we provide and to answer customers' questions

 basic computer skills

 ideally, some experience of cash handling and administrative work.

For more details and an online application form, visit the Vacancies page on our website.

Westerby Leisure Centre
Station Road
Westerby
PT7 9AQ
www.westerbyleisure.co.uk

TEXT B2

Sam received this newsletter by email.

Westerby Leisure Centre
Newsletter – November

Westerby Leisure Centre

Gym

We are pleased to announce that the gym has been completely refurbished and is now open. We have installed a new sound system, new fitness equipment, and given the fitness suite a whole new look. We hope you enjoy using these new, improved facilities.

School Holidays

We are running activity days for 6–12-year-olds throughout the Christmas holidays. Do book early, as our activity days for young people are always very popular. Check our website for details.

Fitness Classes

We are starting some new fitness classes in January. Details are in the timetable below.

January timetable for fitness classes			
	10am–11am	7pm–8pm	8pm–9pm
Monday	Fitness @ 60+	Aerobics	Circuit training
Wednesday	Fitness @ 60+	Aerobics	Circuit training
Friday	Fitness @ 60+	Aerobics	Circuit training
Saturday	Body Blitz	Boxing circuits	Yoga

Each class costs £7 or you can buy a pass to all our classes for a whole week for just £17.

53

TEXT C1

Irenka saw this advert in her local newspaper.

Get the family set for summer!

Our **huge** Summer Sale starts next week.

There are hundreds of bargains to be had in store.
But hurry, these offers are for a limited time only.

These are just some of our amazing offers:

In the womenswear department

A huge range of bikinis, tankinis and all-in-ones from **£14.99**   Flip-flops just **£6.99**   available in blue, cream, pink or purple

---

In the menswear department

Super-comfy, super-tough beach sandals, just **£5.99**   Polo shirts **£4.99** each or **three for £10**

In the children's department

Cartoon T-shirts in a range of colours, just **£3.99**   Shorts for 4–14 year olds, just **£4.99**

Anderson's
the department store
for all the family

The sale is on from 8–22 June. For more details visit us in-store, online, or call us on 0800 600 323

100–110 High Street, Westerby, PT1 8YR

TEXT C2

Irenka has completed this form that she was given in the department store.

Application for Anderson's discount card

Anderson's
the department store
for all the family

Your details

Title	~~Mr / Miss / Mrs~~ / Ms
Name	Irenka Funar
Address	7 Beech Lane, Westerby, PT7 4AU
Telephone number	07796 44392
Email address	irenkaf.96@my.email.com
Date of birth	28th February 1996

Your interests

We would love to know what you're interested in so we can keep you up to date with products you want to hear about. Please tick any of the departments you would like to hear from:

- [ ] menswear
- [x] womenswear
- [ ] children's wear
- [x] beauty
- [ ] toys
- [ ] baby
- [x] electrical
- [ ] sport and leisure
- [ ] furniture

Signed	I. A. Funar
Print name	Irenka Funar
Date	27th June 2017

We would love to keep you informed about new products and special offers.
Please tick the relevant box if you are happy to hear from us by:

- [ ] post
- [ ] text
- [x] email
- [ ] none of the above

Please allow up to 28 days for your card to arrive.
Note: Your discount card cannot be used in conjunction with some other offers. Please see our full terms and conditions at www.andersonsdepartmentstore.co.uk

TASK A1

You have organised an event to raise money for charity.

Write a letter to your local newspaper, asking them to put an article about your event in the newspaper.

You could include:

- why you are writing
- details of the event you have planned
- the charity you are raising money for
- why you think local people will enjoy the event.

Plan and draft your writing before you write your final response.

In your final response, write complete sentences using joining words (conjunctions) e.g. *and, as, but, or.*
Check your spellings.

Remember to use capital letters, full stops and question marks where you need to.

(12 marks)

TASK A2

Your friend spends a lot of time on their mobile phone and laptop. You have planned an activity in your local area to get them away from their phone and laptop for a day.

Write an email to your friend, telling them about the activity you have planned.

You could include:

- details of the activity you have planned
- why you think your friend would enjoy it
- the date and time of the activity
- anything else you think your friend needs to know.

Write complete sentences using joining words (conjunctions) e.g. *and, as, but, or.*

Check your spellings.

Remember to use capital letters, full stops and question marks where you need to.

(8 marks)

TASK B1

You recently bought a tea set online but when it arrived it was damaged.

Write a letter complaining to the company that you bought the item from.

You could include:

• details of the item that you bought
• why you are unhappy with the item
• anything else you think the company needs to know
• what you would like the company to do.

Plan and draft your writing before you write your final response.

In your final response write complete sentences using joining words (conjunctions) e.g. *and, as, but, or*.
Check your spellings.

Remember to use capital letters, full stops and question marks where you need to.

(12 marks)

TASK B2

ESTRICK VOCATIONAL COLLEGE

Your friend wants to take a college course but cannot decide which one to do.

Write an email to your friend, giving them advice about which course to take.

You could include:

- details about the course you are suggesting that your friend should do
- why you think this course would be a good choice for your friend
- anything else you think your friend needs to know.

Write complete sentences using joining words (conjunctions) e.g. *and*, *as*, *but*, *or*.

Check your spellings.

Remember to use capital letters, full stops and question marks where you need to.

(8 marks)

TASK C1

You see this poster pinned up in your local cinema.

Write a letter to Ms Green, applying for this job.

You could include:

- your skills
- any work experience you have
- why you want to work in a cinema
- why you are the perfect person for this job.

Plan and draft your writing before you write your final response.

In your final response write complete sentences using joining words (conjunctions) e.g. *and, as, but, or*. Check your spellings.

Remember to use capital letters, full stops and question marks where you need to.

(12 marks)

TASK C2

Online selling
Sell your old stuff!

Search phrase   Search

Listings

<u>Baby shoes (new and unworn)</u>

More

<u>Signed football</u>

More

<u>Web cam</u>

More

You have decided to sell something that you no longer need, using an online auction site.

Write a notice giving details of the item.

You could include:

• what the item is
• how old the item is and what condition it is in
• why it is useful and people might want to buy it
• anything else you think people would want to know.

Write complete sentences using joining words (conjunctions) e.g. *and, as, but, or*.

Check your spellings.

Remember to use capital letters, full stops and question marks where you need to.

(8 marks)

Answers

READING

1. Your reading test
1 Four
2 20 marks

2. Reading the question
1 B
2 For example: to make larger.

3. Finding the main idea
The text is a poster, advertising the job of receptionist at Westerby Leisure Centre.

4. Underlining key words
1 Every month, check
2 Either: washer fluid levels, or lights

5. Finding details
D

6. Using a dictionary
1 above, animal, machine, movement, statue
2 (a) For example: a climbing plant
  (b) For example: the amount of money needed for a purpose
  (c) For example: leave out or exclude

7. Choosing an answer
B

8. Writing your own answer
Roads in built-up areas such as towns and cities

9. Putting it into practice
In January

10. Headings and sub-headings
A

11. Paragraphs and bullet points
1 Paragraph 1: explains what speed limits are
Paragraph/section 2: gives guidelines for speed limits
Paragraph/section 3: explains what to do if there are no signs
2 C

12. Tables and timetables
B

13. Forms
6 C
7 27th June 2017

14. Putting it into practice
Cartoon T-shirts in a range of colours

WRITING

15. Your writing test
1 Two
2 The first is worth 12 marks, the second is worth 8 marks.
3 45 minutes

16. Reading the question
1 The activity you have planned
2 An email
3 A friend
4 To inform your friend about an activity and persuade them to take part in it

17. Reasons for writing
1 To ask the newspaper to write an article about the event you are organising.
2 You want the newspaper staff to think that their readers would be interested in your event and in the charity you are helping.

18. Who you are writing to
1 The person you are writing to will need details of your order, the reasons why you are unhappy with the item you received, and what you would like them to do about it.
2 Formal language, for example: 'Dear Sir or Madam', 'Yours faithfully'

19. Planning
There is no model answer for this task. Make sure you have:
* included plenty of ideas that cover all the bullet points in the task
* put your ideas in order.

20. Organising
There is no model answer for this task. Make sure you have:
* included plenty of ideas that cover all the bullet points in the task
* put your ideas in order.

21. Drafting
There is no model answer for this task. Make sure you have:
* addressed all the bullet points in the task
* ordered your ideas in paragraphs in a logical order
* written in full sentences in your draft.

22. Checking
Make sure you check your work three times:
* once for spelling
* once for punctuation
* once for sense.

23. Putting it into practice
1 For example: The response answers the question and is well planned and organised. The ideas are relevant to the reader. The response has not been thoroughly checked.
2 Hi Eva

I think you should do a course in construction because it would be really cool for a girl to be a builder. You would learn lots of things. My friend Jamie did the same course and now he's learning bricklaying. He really likes it.

There are always lots of people who need a builder so I think you could get lots of work when you have finished the course. You could make loads of money.

Love

Becca x

3 There is no model answer for this question. Make sure you include all your ideas in a plan and number them in a logical order. Make sure you check your writing for:

- spelling mistakes
- punctuation mistakes
- sentences that do not make clear sense.

24 Writing an email

There is no model answer for this task. Check that your email includes an appropriate greeting and sign-off and appropriate language choices.

25. Writing a letter

The letter should include:

- your address
- the address of the company you ordered the item from
- the date
- the greeting 'Dear Sir or Madam', as you do not know the name of the person you are writing to
- the sign-off 'Yours faithfully', as you do not know the name of the person you are writing to.

26. Writing instructions

There is no model answer for this task. Make sure you have used clear, concise language and presented each step in a logical order.

27. Writing a report

There is no model answer for this task. A good plan will include:

- three or four sub-headings you could use to organise your ideas
- one or two ideas under each sub-heading.

28. Writing a notice or advert

There is no model answer for this task. Make sure you have:

- chosen a heading that will inform and appeal to readers
- included all the key information the reader will need and want to know.

29. Writing a personal statement

There is no model answer for this task. Make sure you include ideas relating to each of the bullet points in the task. Use formal language and add plenty of extra details.

30. Putting it into practice

The letter format is missing:

- the full address of the sender.
- the address of the person to whom it is being sent
- the date.

Some of the language choices in the letter are too informal:

- 'the other day' should be more formally expressed, e.g. 'recently'
- 'I'm' should be written in full: 'I am'
- 'I've' should be written in full: 'I have'
- 'It's' should be written in full: 'It is'
- 'gutted' should be more formally expressed, e.g. 'very disappointed'
- the sign-off should be 'Yours faithfully'.

The email format is too formal:

- 'Dear should' be replaced with an informal greeting, e.g. 'Hi'
- 'Yours sincerely' should be replaced with an informal sign-off, e.g. 'Best wishes'.

31.Paragraphs

1 There is no model answer for this task. Your ideas should cover all the bullet points in the task.

2 You should start a new paragraph every time you introduce a new idea or topic. Use the task bullet points as a guide.

32. Sentences

1 For example:
I have worked every weekend at a local supermarket for two years. I have a lot of experience of serving customers. I am very good at stocking shelves neatly. I have also unloaded large deliveries.

33. Talking about the present

You <u>love</u> going on holiday. You <u>are</u> always good at finding interesting places to visit. I <u>think</u> a course in travel and leisure <u>is</u> perfect for you.

34. Making the verb match

1 & 3 A <u>I love</u> playing football for my local team.

B <u>We were</u> first in our league last season.

C <u>Our manager trains</u> us every week and <u>we work</u> hard for him.

D <u>The whole team loves</u> him.

2 The following verbs are incorrect: B (was), C (train), D (love)

35. Talking about the past

1 I <u>tried</u> my best in my job. I <u>worked</u> hard. I never <u>stopped</u> trying and I always <u>found</u> solutions to problems. My ambition <u>was</u> to become a manager.

36. Talking about the future

1 I will try my best in my job. I will work hard. I will never stop trying and I will always find solutions to problems. My ambition will be to become a manager.

37. Using joining words

For example:

I really like to eat Mexican and Indian food.

My dad likes football but he doesn't like rugby.

He will go for a run when the sun comes out.

We will go to the cinema because it is my birthday.

She dances all the time but she is not very good.

38. Putting it into practice

There is no model answer for this question. Make sure you are confident with this topic. Ask your teacher to for help if you are unsure.

39. Capital letters

75 Long Lane

Missleford

RB7 6RR

5th January 2017

Dear Ms Green

I am writing to apply for the job at Westerby Picture Palace. I have lots of experience of stocking shelves and serving customers as I have been working at Westerby Petrol Station for the past two months. It would be great to work in a cinema because I love films.

Yours sincerely

Aran White

40. Ending a sentence

I bought a mobile phone from you last week. It does not work. I cannot get a signal anywhere. It will not connect to wi-fi. Would you please let me know how I can get a refund? Thank you.

41. Putting it into practice

19 May 2017

Dear Sir or Madam

I bought a tea set from your website and when it arrived it was broken.

- The saucers are chipped.
- There are sharp edges on the cups.
- The tea pot doesn't pour properly.

I want to change it for a new one please. Could you tell me where I should send it?

Yours faithfully

Chantelle Grundy

42. Spelling tips

Make a list of spellings you find tricky and practise them regularly before the test.

43. Plurals

1 He trys/tries to put healthy lunchs/lunches in his children's lunchboxs/lunchboxes every day.

2 She sits on one of the benches/benchs in the park eating her sandwichs/sandwiches.

3 I have happy memories/memorys of my journies/journeys to London.

44. Prefixes

- For example: unhappy, untrue, unsure
- For example: misread, mistake, misunderstand

45. Suffixes

There is no model answers for this question. Make sure you are familiar with the suffixes mentioned on page 45.

46. Tricky spellings 1

1 I found out where/were they where/were going.

2 They're/there going they're/there later.

3 Lots of/off people are heading of/off on holiday.

4 They're/Their not sure where/were they lost they're/their money.

5 I worked in a company where/were there where/were alot/a lot of/off other young people.

47. Tricky spellings 2

1 Two/too people brought/bought a cake to/too college.

2 I was too/to full too/to eat any.

3 Are/Our you going too/to eat some know/now?

4 I have got know/no idea if I brought/bought them home or left them behind.

5 I know/no what I should have/should of done.

48. Tricky spellings 3

Make a list of spellings you find tricky and practise them regularly before the test.

49. Putting it into practice

Hi Marin

I heard you were thinking of going to college and wanted to know what course to do. I think you should do a course in retail because you would be brilliant at running a shop. You are great at chatting to people. There are loads of different kinds of shops. It's your decision!

I know I should have thought of this before but there hasn't been much time because I've been too busy at college. I've been rushed off my feet. Sorry!

Best wishes

Gov

Notes

Notes

Notes

Notes

Notes

Published by Pearson Education Limited, 80 Strand, London, WC2R 0RL.

www.pearsonschoolsandfecolleges.co.uk

Copies of official specifications for all Edexcel qualifications may be found on the website: www.edexcel.com

Text © Pearson Education Limited 2017
Edited, typeset and produced by Elektra Media Ltd
Original illustrations © Pearson Education Limited 2017
Illustrated by Elektra Media Ltd
Cover illustration by Miriam Sturdee

The right of David Grant to be identified as author of this work has been asserted by him in accordance with the Copyright, Designs and Patents Act 1988.

First published 2017

20 19 18 17
10 9 8 7 6 5 4 3 2 1

British Library Cataloguing in Publication Data
A catalogue record for this book is available from the British Library

ISBN 978 1 292 20711 7

Printed in Slovakia by Neografia.

A note from the publisher
In order to ensure that this resource offers high-quality support for the associated Pearson qualification, it has been through a review process by the awarding body. This process confirms that this resource fully covers the teaching and learning content of the specification or part of a specification at which it is aimed. It also confirms that it demonstrates an appropriate balance between the development of subject skills, knowledge and understanding, in addition to preparation for assessment.

Endorsement does not cover any guidance on assessment activities or processes (e.g. practice questions or advice on how to answer assessment questions), included in the resource nor does it prescribe any particular approach to the teaching or delivery of a related course.

While the publishers have made every attempt to ensure that advice on the qualification and its assessment is accurate, the official specification and associated assessment guidance materials are the only authoritative source of information and should always be referred to for definitive guidance.

Pearson examiners have not contributed to any sections in this resource relevant to examination papers for which they have responsibility.

Examiners will not use endorsed resources as a source of material for any assessment set by Pearson. Endorsement of a resource does not mean that the resource is required to achieve this Pearson qualification, nor does it mean that it is the only suitable material available to support the qualification, and any resource lists produced by the awarding body shall include this and other appropriate resources.